All rights reserved
978-1-7394545-0-0
First impression, 2023
Wooden House Books
www.woodenhousebooks.com

This Kindness book belongs to

_ _

The Kids' Book of
KINDNESS

Catherine Stephenson. Illustrated by Hiruni Kariyawasam.

Emotions, Empathy and How to Be Kind

What is kindness?

Kindness is many things.

We are kind when we do things to help others and make them feel good. It could be sharing a snack, giving a hug to someone who is sad or upset, or helping someone with a problem.

We can also be kind to animals and the environment.

Kindness is even about being loving and thoughtful to ourselves.

Kindness makes other people feel happy and appreciated.

Can you think of a time someone was kind to you? Maybe a time that somebody helped, encouraged, comforted or included you?

Can you describe how you felt?

Being kind to others can make you feel good too!

Can you think of a time when you did something kind for someone, or made them smile? How did it make you feel?

When you make someone
else's day a little bit brighter,
it can make you feel happy too!

Kindness is noticing feelings.

sad

happy

angry

scared

worried

bored

Can you think of times you have had any
of these feelings? Noticing your feelings can
help you take care of yourself.

It is also important to notice how others
are feeling. It helps us to be more
understanding. Are they feeling sad, upset,
frightened or finding something difficult?

What could you do to help them feel better?
Could you listen to them? Tell them a story
to cheer them up? Help them to do something?

You can express kindness in many ways

Some people like giving and receiving hugs and cuddles, others prefer a fist bump.

You can use kind words and speak gently.

drawing a picture for someone

helping tidy up

offering your help

And you can show kindness by actions such as listening, sharing, helping someone, or doing something nice for someone.

reading to someone

spending time chatting to someone

telling someone a joke to make them laugh

Kindness is being responsible.

laying the table

giving away your old things

It's kind to take care of things, people and places.
To think about how your actions affect other people
and trying to make things better for everyone.

For example, if you clean up your toys after playing, it
means others won't have to do it or won't trip over them.

hanging up your coat

throwing your litter away

tidying up your toys

Kindness is also taking care of other
people's feelings. Listening to your parents
or carers, teachers, and friends shows you
care what they have to say.

Kindness is including.

No matter who we are or where we
come from, we are all unique and special
in our own way!

If you see someone who is alone or not
included in a game, ask them if they want to
join. This helps them feel part of things.

Celebrate people's differences by learning
about different cultures, traditions, and
ways of life. Help build a world where
everyone feels loved and accepted!

saying hi to
someone.

working with
someone new

being a good
listener

smiling

Friends are kind.

Kindness is an important part of friendship because it helps us show we care.

When we are kind to our friends, we make them feel happy, valued, and loved.

Being kind shows you care about someone,
and can help make new friends too!

If you see a child who looks sad, you could
go and say hello or ask if they're okay.

Kindness is doing what is right and fair.

Kindness is about being a good person and a good friend. Helping people, being respectful, sharing and being fair.

Nobody gets it right all the time. If you make a mistake or hurt someone's feelings, try and say sorry. Saying sorry is also a type of kindness.

Doing what is right can sometimes be hard, but it is important to be brave and speak up for what you believe in.

This might mean standing up to someone who is being mean to others, telling the truth even if it is difficult, or doing the right thing even if no one else is doing it.

You can be kind and still say "no".

Being kind doesn't mean you have to do everything that someone else wants you to do, or agree with everything they say. It's important to be honest about your own opinions and feelings.

Sometimes, people might say or do things that you don't think are right or fair. Try to speak up — you can do it in a kind way, by listening to what they have to say, and sharing your ideas respectfully.

Choose kindness whenever possible.

Sometimes, people might say or do mean things. It can be hard, but try and be kind back, and treat them with respect and caring.

It's always better to try to resolve
conflicts peacefully and with kindness,
rather than with more anger and meanness.

Kindness is very powerful — it can even help
to turn a difficult situation into a good one.

Be kind to animals.

Animals are living beings just like us, and deserve our kindness and respect. Always be gentle when you touch or play with animals. If an animal seems scared or uncomfortable, give them some space. Be kind to all animals, big and small.

You can learn more about different animals and their needs by reading books or watching videos.

If you see an animal that looks hurt or in danger, tell a trusted adult right away.

Be kind to nature.

The Earth gives us clean air to breathe, water to drink, food to eat, and special places like rivers, mountains, beaches and woods.

There are lots of ways to show kindness to nature.

Can you think of anything that you do to care for the earth?

saving water

observing wildlife

looking after plants

picking up litter

planting a tree

Connect with nature. Find a nature trail or wild place near you where you can observe plants, trees, water, or creatures.

Climb a tree! Jump in a pile of leaves! Splash in a puddle or roll in the mud!

Most important of all,
be kind to yourself.

You deserve the very same love
and care that you give to others.

Being kind to yourself is
taking care of your body,
things like eating healthy food
and getting enough sleep.

It's also doing things you enjoy.

What do you like doing that makes you feel happy and relaxed?

Maybe it's reading, drawing, listening to music or doing a sport.

Be gentle with yourself when you make mistakes.

And ask for help when you need it — we all need support sometimes.

Turn the world kind.

Even small acts of kindness can have a big impact on the world around us.

Maybe you pick up a toy for a friend who dropped it, or say hello to someone new. That might make them feel happy and appreciated, and they might do something kind for someone else. You never know how far your kindness will travel.

Imagine a world filled with kindness...
Wouldn't that be fantastic?!

An Act of Kindness

Draw a picture of a time when someone was kind to you (or you were kind to someone else).

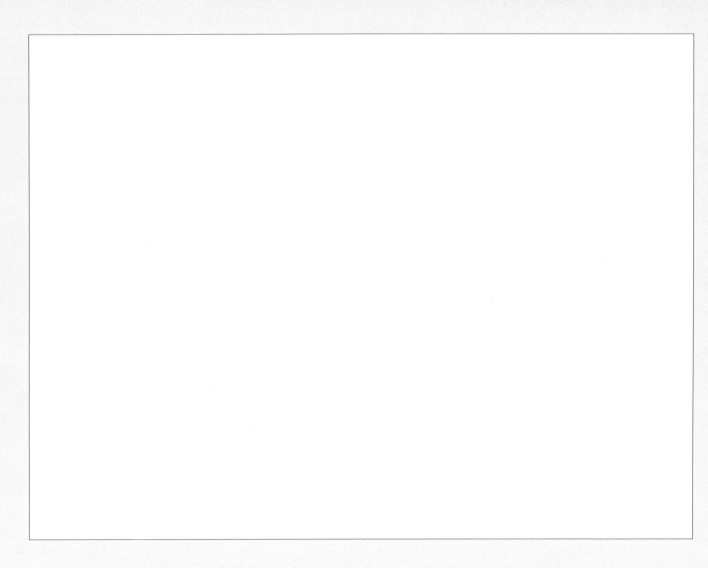

having a
bubble bath

talking
positively
to yourself when
you make a
mistake

listening
to music

meditation

cuddling your
favourite teddy

Being Kind to Yourself

When we think about being kind, we often
think about helping others. But being kind
to ourselves is just as important.

Here are some ideas for things you could
do. Can you think of anything that makes
YOU feel happy, healthy, and calm?

dancing in the
kitchen

coloring a
mandala

getting lots
of sleep

a hug with
someone
you love

taking a break
when you're
feeling tired

running,
skipping or
jumping!

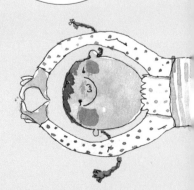

Kindness Counter

Every time you do a kind deed, you brighten someone else's day a little bit. Color one heart for every kind thing you do for others.

Be a Kindness Superhero!

Think of 3 Kindness SuperHero missions and carry them out. You can choose from the ideas below, or why not think of your own?

MISSION 1 _____ _____

MISSION 2 _____ _____

MISSION 3 _____ _____   POW!

really listen to someone

invite someone to join your game

tell someone you appreciate them

smile at someone

hold a door open for someone

offer to help with a chore

pick up some litter

sit with a new friend at lunch

ask someone if they need help

Problem-solving with Kindness

Read each problem carefully and think about how you can solve it with kindness. Write your solution in the space provided.

1. A classmate borrowed your pencil and hasn't returned it.

_____

_____

2. You see someone being teased by other kids.

_____

_____

3. You and your brother or sister both want to play with the same toy.

_____

_____

4. A new student joins your class and seems shy.

_____

_____

Kind or not kind?

Decide if these things are kind or not kind and tick the right box.

Kind | Not kind

☐ ☐ 1. Recycling your paper and plastic.

☐ ☐ 2. Ignoring someone who says hello to you.

☐ ☐ 3. Helping a classmate with their homework.

☐ ☐ 4. Saying "please" and "thank you."

☐ ☐ 5. Making fun of someone's clothes.

☐ ☐ 6. Interrupting when someone else is talking.

☐ ☐ 7. Holding the door open for others.

☐ ☐ 8. Laughing at someone who made a mistake.

☐ ☐ 9. Blaming someone else for something you did.

☐ ☐ 10. Cleaning up after your pet.

Dear Reader,

Thank you for choosing to read *The Kids' Book of Kindness* with your child – we hope you enjoyed it.

If you have a few moments to leave a review online, we would greatly appreciate it. As a small independent publisher, reviews make a big difference in helping others discover our books. Simply scan the QR code to go directly to the review page on Amazon.com.

This book forms part of The Kids' Books of Social Emotional Learning series, which also includes:

Thank you so much for your interest and support!

Catherine
woodenhousebooks.com

About the author and the illustrator.

Catherine (author)

Catherine was born in the UK and grew up in Wales. She now lives with her partner, son and two cats in Barcelona. She is a freelance writer and translator from Spanish and Catalan into English. Her other books include *The Kids' Book of Friends* and the dual language book *Alice and the White Rabbit*. Away from work, you'll find her in the mountains with a camera round her neck.

Hiruni (illustrator)

Hiruni is from Sri Lanka, where she lives with her family in a town called Ambalangoda. She holds a Bachelor's Degree in Fashion Design from the Univversity of Moratuwa. She enjoys doing paintings, fine illustrations, and especially illustrations for children's books in her unique style, mixing digital and watercolour techniques. In her free time, she's also an avid reader.

You can find us at:

WOODEN HOUSE BOOKS

woodenhousebooks.com
IG @woodenhousebooks

Made in United States
Troutdale, OR
11/30/2024

25385529R00026